AF225440

# This Book Belongs To:

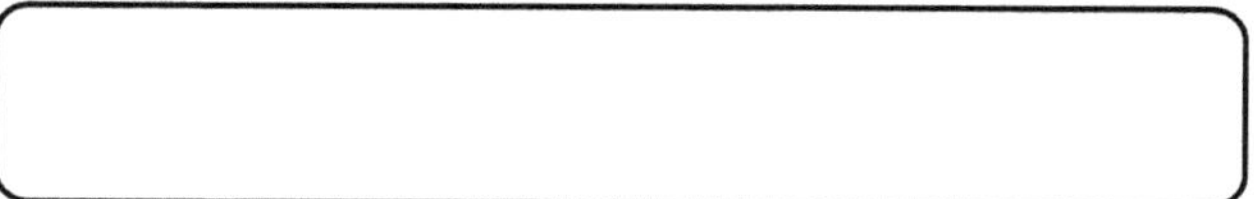

**Day**            **Date**

:           :

## I am thankful for:

1. _______________________________________

2. _______________________________________

3. _______________________________________

**Who has made you happy today:**

## Today I feel:

## Write or draw anything about today

| **Day** | **Date** |
| --- | --- |
| : | : |

## I am thankful for:

1. __________________________________________

2. __________________________________________

3. __________________________________________

**Who has made you happy today:**

## Today I feel:

## Write or draw anything about today

**Day**          **Date**

:          :

## I am thankful for:

1. _______________________________________

2. _______________________________________

3. _______________________________________

**Who has made you happy today:**

## Today I feel:

## Write or draw anything about today

<table><tr><td>**Day**</td><td>**Date**</td></tr><tr><td>:</td><td>:</td></tr></table>

## I am thankful for:

☆1 ________________________________

☆2 ________________________________

☆3 ________________________________

**Who has made you happy today:**

## Today I feel:

## Write or draw anything about today

| **Day** | **Date** |
| : | : |

## I am thankful for:

☆1☆ ________________________________

☆2☆ ________________________________

☆3☆ ________________________________

**Who has made you happy today:**

## Today I feel:

## Write or draw anything about today

<table><tr><td>**Day**</td><td>**Date**</td></tr><tr><td>:</td><td>:</td></tr></table>

## I am thankful for:

1. ________________________________

2. ________________________________

3. ________________________________

**Who has made you happy today:**

## Today I feel:

## Write or draw anything about today

| **Day** | **Date** |
| : | : |

## I am thankful for:

☆1☆ ______________________________

☆2☆ ______________________________

☆3☆ ______________________________

**Who has made you happy today:**

## Today I feel:

## Write or draw anything about today

| **Day** | **Date** |
| : | : |

## I am thankful for:

1 ______________________________

2 ______________________________

3 ______________________________

## Who has made you happy today:

## Today I feel:

## Write or draw anything about today

| **Day** | **Date** |
| : | : |

## I am thankful for:

★ 1 ______________________________

★ 2 ______________________________

★ 3 ______________________________

**Who has made you happy today:**

## Today I feel:

## Write or draw anything about today

| **Day** | **Date** |
| : | : |

## I am thankful for:

☆1 ________________________________

☆2 ________________________________

☆3 ________________________________

**Who has made you happy today:**

## Today I feel:

## Write or draw anything about today

<table><tr><td>**Day**</td><td>**Date**</td></tr></table>

## I am thankful for:

1. _______________________________

2. _______________________________

3. _______________________________

**Who has made you happy today:**

## Today I feel:

## Write or draw anything about today

<table>
<tr><td>Day</td><td>Date</td></tr>
<tr><td>:</td><td>:</td></tr>
</table>

## I am thankful for:

1. ____________________________________________

2. ____________________________________________

3. ____________________________________________

## Who has made you happy today:

## Today I feel:

## Write or draw anything about today

Day          Date

:         :

## I am thankful for:

1. __________________________________________

2. __________________________________________

3. __________________________________________

**Who has made you happy today:**

## Today I feel:

**Write or draw anything about today**

<table><tr><td>**Day**</td><td>**Date**</td></tr></table>

## I am thankful for:

1. _______________________________________
2. _______________________________________
3. _______________________________________

## Who has made you happy today:

## Today I feel:

## Write or draw anything about today

<table><tr><td>**Day**</td><td>**Date**</td></tr></table>

## I am thankful for:

1. __________________________________________

2. __________________________________________

3. __________________________________________

## Who has made you happy today:

## Today I feel:

## Write or draw anything about today

<table><tr><td>**Day**</td><td>**Date**</td></tr></table>

## I am thankful for:

⭐ **1** ___________________________________________

⭐ **2** ___________________________________________

⭐ **3** ___________________________________________

## Who has made you happy today:

## Today I feel:

## Write or draw anything about today

| **Day** | **Date** |
| :--- | :--- |

## I am thankful for:

⭐ 1 ______________________________

⭐ 2 ______________________________

⭐ 3 ______________________________

**Who has made you happy today:**

## Today I feel:

**Write or draw anything about today**

<table><tr><td>**Day**</td><td>**Date**</td></tr></table>

## I am thankful for:

1. _______________________

2. _______________________

3. _______________________

**Who has made you happy today:**

## Today I feel:

## Write or draw anything about today

| Day | Date |
|---|---|
| : | : |

## I am thankful for:

1. __________________________________________

2. __________________________________________

3. __________________________________________

**Who has made you happy today:**

## Today I feel:

## Write or draw anything about today

| **Day** | **Date** |
| :--- | :--- |

## I am thankful for:

⭐ **1** ______________________________________

⭐ **2** ______________________________________

⭐ **3** ______________________________________

## Who has made you happy today:

## Today I feel:

## Write or draw anything about today

<table>
<tr><td>Day</td><td>Date</td></tr>
<tr><td>:</td><td>:</td></tr>
</table>

## I am thankful for:

1. ________________________________________

2. ________________________________________

3. ________________________________________

**Who has made you happy today:**

## Today I feel:

## Write or draw anything about today

| **Day** | **Date** |
| --- | --- |
| : | : |

## I am thankful for:

☆1 ____________________________________

☆2 ____________________________________

☆3 ____________________________________

**Who has made you happy today:**

## Today I feel:

## Write or draw anything about today

<table><tr><td>**Day**</td><td>**Date**</td></tr><tr><td>:</td><td>:</td></tr></table>

## I am thankful for:

1. ______________________________

2. ______________________________

3. ______________________________

**Who has made you happy today:**

## Today I feel:

## Write or draw anything about today

| **Day** | **Date** |
| :--- | :--- |

## I am thankful for:

☆1 ______________________________

☆2 ______________________________

☆3 ______________________________

## Who has made you happy today:

## Today I feel:

## Write or draw anything about today

<table>
<tr><td>Day</td><td>Date</td></tr>
<tr><td>:</td><td>:</td></tr>
</table>

## I am thankful for:

1. ______________________________________
2. ______________________________________
3. ______________________________________

## Who has made you happy today:

## Today I feel:

## Write or draw anything about today

| **Day** | **Date** |
| :--- | :--- |

## I am thankful for:

☆1 ______________________________

☆2 ______________________________

☆3 ______________________________

**Who has made you happy today:**

## Today I feel:

## Write or draw anything about today

<table><tr><td>**Day**</td><td>**Date**</td></tr></table>

: :

## I am thankful for:

1. ______________________________

2. ______________________________

3. ______________________________

**Who has made you happy today:**

## Today I feel:

😃 😉 😐 🙁 ☹️

## Write or draw anything about today

| **Day** | **Date** |
| :--- | :--- |

## I am thankful for:

⭐ **1** ______________________________________

⭐ **2** ______________________________________

⭐ **3** ______________________________________

## Who has made you happy today:

## Today I feel:

## Write or draw anything about today

| **Day** | **Date** |
| :--- | :--- |

## I am thankful for:

1. _______________________________

2. _______________________________

3. _______________________________

**Who has made you happy today:**

## Today I feel:

## Write or draw anything about today

<table><tr><td>**Day**</td><td>**Date**</td></tr><tr><td>:</td><td>:</td></tr></table>

## I am thankful for:

1. __________________________________________

2. __________________________________________

3. __________________________________________

## Who has made you happy today:

## Today I feel:

## Write or draw anything about today

| **Day** | **Date** |
| : | : |

## I am thankful for:

☆**1** ________________________________

☆**2** ________________________________

☆**3** ________________________________

**Who has made you happy today:**

## Today I feel:

## Write or draw anything about today

| **Day** | **Date** |
| --- | --- |
| : | : |

## I am thankful for:

⭐ 1 _______________________________

⭐ 2 _______________________________

⭐ 3 _______________________________

**Who has made you happy today:**

## Today I feel:

## Write or draw anything about today

| **Day** | **Date** |
| : | : |

## I am thankful for:

⭐1 ____________________________________

⭐2 ____________________________________

⭐3 ____________________________________

**Who has made you happy today:**

## Today I feel:

## Write or draw anything about today

<table><tr><td>Day</td><td>Date</td></tr></table>

## I am thankful for:

1. ___________________________________________

2. ___________________________________________

3. ___________________________________________

## Who has made you happy today:

## Today I feel:

## Write or draw anything about today

| **Day** | **Date** |
| :--- | :--- |

## I am thankful for:

☆1 ______________________________________

★2 ______________________________________

☆3 ______________________________________

**Who has made you happy today:**

## Today I feel:

## Write or draw anything about today

<table><tr><td>**Day**</td><td>**Date**</td></tr></table>

## I am thankful for:

1. ___________________________

2. ___________________________

3. ___________________________

## Who has made you happy today:

## Today I feel:

## Write or draw anything about today

**Day**        **Date**

:         :

## I am thankful for:

1. ____________________________________

2. ____________________________________

3. ____________________________________

**Who has made you happy today:**

## Today I feel:

**Write or draw anything about today**

| **Day** | **Date** |
| :--- | :--- |

## I am thankful for:

☆1 _______________________________________

☆2 _______________________________________

☆3 _______________________________________

## Who has made you happy today:

## Today I feel:

## Write or draw anything about today

| Day | Date |

**Day :**

**Date :**

## I am thankful for:

1. ___________________________________

2. ___________________________________

3. ___________________________________

## Who has made you happy today:

## Today I feel:

## Write or draw anything about today

**Day**        **Date**

:                 :

## I am thankful for:

1. ___________________________________

2. ___________________________________

3. ___________________________________

**Who has made you happy today:**

## Today I feel:

## Write or draw anything about today

<table><tr><td>**Day**</td><td>**Date**</td></tr><tr><td>:</td><td>:</td></tr></table>

## I am thankful for:

1. __________________________________________

2. __________________________________________

3. __________________________________________

**Who has made you happy today:**

## Today I feel:

## Write or draw anything about today

| **Day** | **Date** |
| : | : |

## I am thankful for:

1 ______________________________________

2 ______________________________________

3 ______________________________________

**Who has made you happy today:**

## Today I feel:

## Write or draw anything about today

| **Day** | **Date** |
| :--- | :--- |

## I am thankful for:

☆1 ______________________________________

☆2 ______________________________________

☆3 ______________________________________

**Who has made you happy today:**

## Today I feel:

## Write or draw anything about today

| **Day** | **Date** |
| --- | --- |
| : | : |

## I am thankful for:

1. ______________________________________________

2. ______________________________________________

3. ______________________________________________

## Who has made you happy today:

## Today I feel:

## Write or draw anything about today

<table><tr><td>**Day**</td><td>**Date**</td></tr><tr><td>:</td><td>:</td></tr></table>

## I am thankful for:

1. _______________________________________________

2. _______________________________________________

3. _______________________________________________

**Who has made you happy today:**

## Today I feel:

## Write or draw anything about today

<table><tr><td>**Day**</td><td>**Date**</td></tr></table>

## I am thankful for:

⭐ 1 ______________________________

⭐ 2 ______________________________

⭐ 3 ______________________________

**Who has made you happy today:**

## Today I feel:

## Write or draw anything about today

| **Day** | **Date** |
| :--- | :--- |

## I am thankful for:

☆1 ______________________________

☆2 ______________________________

☆3 ______________________________

**Who has made you happy today:**

## Today I feel:

## Write or draw anything about today

<table><tr><td>Day</td><td>Date</td></tr><tr><td>:</td><td>:</td></tr></table>

## I am thankful for:

1. ___________________________________________

2. ___________________________________________

3. ___________________________________________

## Who has made you happy today:

## Today I feel:

## Write or draw anything about today

<table><tr><td>**Day**</td><td>**Date**</td></tr><tr><td>:</td><td>:</td></tr></table>

## I am thankful for:

1. ______________________________

2. ______________________________

3. ______________________________

## Who has made you happy today:

## Today I feel:

## Write or draw anything about today

**Day**          **Date**

:          :

## I am thankful for:

1. __________________________

2. __________________________

3. __________________________

**Who has made you happy today:**

## Today I feel:

## Write or draw anything about today

| **Day** | **Date** |
| :--- | :--- |

## I am thankful for:

1. __________________________________________

2. __________________________________________

3. __________________________________________

**Who has made you happy today:**

## Today I feel:

## Write or draw anything about today

<table><tr><td>**Day**</td><td>**Date**</td></tr></table>

## I am thankful for:

☆1 ______________________________

☆2 ______________________________

☆3 ______________________________

**Who has made you happy today:**

## Today I feel:

## Write or draw anything about today

<table>
<tr><td>Day</td><td>Date</td></tr>
<tr><td>:</td><td>:</td></tr>
</table>

## I am thankful for:

1. __________________________

2. __________________________

3. __________________________

## Who has made you happy today:

## Today I feel:

## Write or draw anything about today

| **Day** | **Date** |
| : | : |

## I am thankful for:

☆1 ________________________________

☆2 ________________________________

☆3 ________________________________

## Who has made you happy today:

## Today I feel:

## Write or draw anything about today

| **Day** | **Date** |
| :--- | :--- |

## I am thankful for:

1. ______________________________________
2. ______________________________________
3. ______________________________________

**Who has made you happy today:**

## Today I feel:

## Write or draw anything about today

| Day | Date |
|---|---|
| : | : |

## I am thankful for:

⭐ **1** ______________________________

⭐ **2** ______________________________

⭐ **3** ______________________________

**Who has made you happy today:**

## Today I feel:

## Write or draw anything about today

| Day | Date |
| --- | --- |
| : | : |

## I am thankful for:

☆1 _______________________________

☆2 _______________________________

☆3 _______________________________

**Who has made you happy today:**

## Today I feel:

## Write or draw anything about today

**Day**

**Date**

**I am thankful for:**

1. ______________________________
2. ______________________________
3. ______________________________

**Who has made you happy today:**

**Today I feel:**

**Write or draw anything about today**

| Day | Date |
| --- | --- |
| : | : |

## I am thankful for:

⭐ 1 ______________________________

⭐ 2 ______________________________

⭐ 3 ______________________________

**Who has made you happy today:**

## Today I feel:

## Write or draw anything about today

<table>
<tr><td>Day</td><td>Date</td></tr>
<tr><td>:</td><td>:</td></tr>
</table>

## I am thankful for:

1. _______________________________
2. _______________________________
3. _______________________________

## Who has made you happy today:

## Today I feel:

## Write or draw anything about today

<table><tr><td>**Day**</td><td>**Date**</td></tr></table>

## I am thankful for:

1. _______________________________________

2. _______________________________________

3. _______________________________________

**Who has made you happy today:**

## Today I feel:

## Write or draw anything about today

| **Day** | **Date** |
|---|---|
| : | : |

## I am thankful for:

⭐ 1 _______________________________________

⭐ 2 _______________________________________

⭐ 3 _______________________________________

**Who has made you happy today:**

## Today I feel:

## Write or draw anything about today

| **Day** | **Date** |
| :-- | :-- |

## I am thankful for:

⭐ 1 _______________________________

⭐ 2 _______________________________

⭐ 3 _______________________________

**Who has made you happy today:**

## Today I feel:

## Write or draw anything about today

| **Day** | **Date** |
| :--- | :--- |

## I am thankful for:

1. _______________________________

2. _______________________________

3. _______________________________

**Who has made you happy today:**

## Today I feel:

## Write or draw anything about today

| **Day** | **Date** |
| --- | --- |
| : | : |

## I am thankful for:

☆1 ____________________________________

☆2 ____________________________________

☆3 ____________________________________

**Who has made you happy today:**

## Today I feel:

## Write or draw anything about today

<table><tr><td>**Day**</td><td>**Date**</td></tr><tr><td>:</td><td>:</td></tr></table>

## I am thankful for:

1. ______________________________

2. ______________________________

3. ______________________________

## Who has made you happy today:

## Today I feel:

## Write or draw anything about today

<table><tr><td>Day</td><td>Date</td></tr><tr><td>:</td><td>:</td></tr></table>

## I am thankful for:

1. __________________________________________

2. __________________________________________

3. __________________________________________

## Who has made you happy today:

## Today I feel:

## Write or draw anything about today

**Day**           **Date**

:           :

## I am thankful for:

1. _______________________________________________

2. _______________________________________________

3. _______________________________________________

**Who has made you happy today:**

## Today I feel:

## Write or draw anything about today

<table><tr><td>**Day**</td><td>**Date**</td></tr></table>

:                           :

## I am thankful for:

1 _______________________________

2 _______________________________

3 _______________________________

**Who has made you happy today:**

## Today I feel:

**Write or draw anything about today**

| **Day** | **Date** |
| :--- | :--- |

## I am thankful for:

☆1 _________________________________

☆2 _________________________________

☆3 _________________________________

**Who has made you happy today:**

## Today I feel:

## Write or draw anything about today

<table><tr><td>**Day**</td><td>**Date**</td></tr></table>

## I am thankful for:

1. __________________________________________

2. __________________________________________

3. __________________________________________

**Who has made you happy today:**

## Today I feel:

## Write or draw anything about today

| **Day** | **Date** |
| :--- | :--- |

## I am thankful for:

1. __________________________________________
2. __________________________________________
3. __________________________________________

## Who has made you happy today:

## Today I feel:

## Write or draw anything about today

<table><tr><td>**Day**</td><td>**Date**</td></tr></table>

## I am thankful for:

1. ______________________________

2. ______________________________

3. ______________________________

**Who has made you happy today:**

## Today I feel:

## Write or draw anything about today

| **Day** | **Date** |
| :--- | :--- |

## I am thankful for:

1. _______________________________________________
2. _______________________________________________
3. _______________________________________________

**Who has made you happy today:**

## Today I feel:

## Write or draw anything about today

| **Day** | **Date** |
| :--- | :--- |

## I am thankful for:

☆1 ______________________________________

☆2 ______________________________________

☆3 ______________________________________

**Who has made you happy today:**

## Today I feel:

## Write or draw anything about today

| **Day** | **Date** |

**I am thankful for:**

⭐ 1 ______________________________

⭐ 2 ______________________________

⭐ 3 ______________________________

**Who has made you happy today:**

**Today I feel:**

**Write or draw anything about today**

<table><tr><td>Day</td><td>Date</td></tr><tr><td>:</td><td>:</td></tr></table>

## I am thankful for:

1. ______________________________________________

2. ______________________________________________

3. ______________________________________________

**Who has made you happy today:**

## Today I feel:

## Write or draw anything about today

<table><tr><td>**Day**</td><td>**Date**</td></tr><tr><td>:</td><td>:</td></tr></table>

## I am thankful for:

1. _______________________________________________

2. _______________________________________________

3. _______________________________________________

## Who has made you happy today:

## Today I feel:

## Write or draw anything about today

<table><tr><td>**Day**</td><td>**Date**</td></tr></table>

## I am thankful for:

1. __________________________________________

2. __________________________________________

3. __________________________________________

**Who has made you happy today:**

## Today I feel:

## Write or draw anything about today

| **Day** | **Date** |
| : | : |

## I am thankful for:

1. _______________________________________

2. _______________________________________

3. _______________________________________

**Who has made you happy today:**

## Today I feel:

## Write or draw anything about today

<table><tr><td>**Day**</td><td>**Date**</td></tr></table>

## I am thankful for:

1. _______________________________

2. _______________________________

3. _______________________________

**Who has made you happy today:**

## Today I feel:

## Write or draw anything about today

<table><tr><td>**Day**</td><td>**Date**</td></tr></table>

## I am thankful for:

1. ___________________________________________

2. ___________________________________________

3. ___________________________________________

## Who has made you happy today:

## Today I feel:

## Write or draw anything about today

| **Day** | **Date** |
| :--- | :--- |

## I am thankful for:

1. ______________________________
2. ______________________________
3. ______________________________

**Who has made you happy today:**

## Today I feel:

## Write or draw anything about today

| **Day** | **Date** |
| :--- | :--- |

## I am thankful for:

★ 1 ____________________________________________

★ 2 ____________________________________________

★ 3 ____________________________________________

**Who has made you happy today:**

## Today I feel:

## Write or draw anything about today

**Day**     **Date**

:            :

## I am thankful for:

☆1☆ _______________________________________

☆2☆ _______________________________________

☆3☆ _______________________________________

**Who has made you happy today:**

## Today I feel:

### Write or draw anything about today

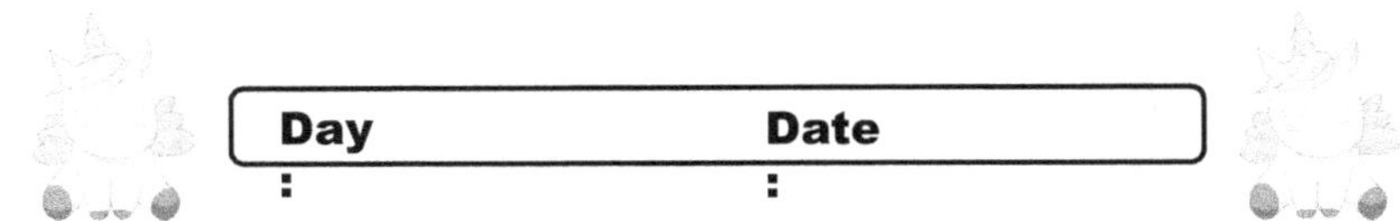

| Day | Date |
| --- | --- |
| : | : |

## I am thankful for:

1. ___________________________________

2. ___________________________________

3. ___________________________________

**Who has made you happy today:**

## Today I feel:

## Write or draw anything about today

| **Day** | **Date** |
| : | : |

## I am thankful for:

1. ________________________________________

2. ________________________________________

3. ________________________________________

**Who has made you happy today:**

## Today I feel:

## Write or draw anything about today

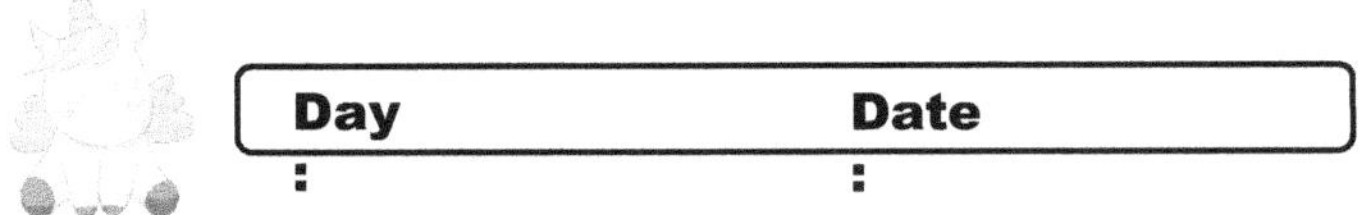

| **Day** | **Date** |
|---|---|
| : | : |

## I am thankful for:

⭐ 1 ____________________________________________

⭐ 2 ____________________________________________

⭐ 3 ____________________________________________

## Who has made you happy today:

## Today I feel:

## Write or draw anything about today

<table><tr><td>**Day**</td><td>**Date**</td></tr><tr><td>:</td><td>:</td></tr></table>

## I am thankful for:

1. ___________________________________
2. ___________________________________
3. ___________________________________

**Who has made you happy today:**

## Today I feel:

## Write or draw anything about today

<table><tr><td>**Day**</td><td>**Date**</td></tr></table>

## I am thankful for:

⭐ 1 _______________________

⭐ 2 _______________________

⭐ 3 _______________________

**Who has made you happy today:**

## Today I feel:

## Write or draw anything about today

<table><tr><td>**Day**</td><td>**Date**</td></tr><tr><td>:</td><td>:</td></tr></table>

## I am thankful for:

1. ______________________________

2. ______________________________

3. ______________________________

**Who has made you happy today:**

## Today I feel:

## Write or draw anything about today

<table><tr><td>Day</td><td>Date</td></tr><tr><td>:</td><td>:</td></tr></table>

## I am thankful for:

1. ______________________________

2. ______________________________

3. ______________________________

**Who has made you happy today:**

## Today I feel:

## Write or draw anything about today

<table><tr><td>**Day**</td><td>**Date**</td></tr><tr><td>:</td><td>:</td></tr></table>

## I am thankful for:

1. __________________________________________

2. __________________________________________

3. __________________________________________

## Who has made you happy today:

## Today I feel:

## Write or draw anything about today

| **Day** | **Date** |
| :--- | :--- |

## I am thankful for:

1. __________________________________________

2. __________________________________________

3. __________________________________________

**Who has made you happy today:**

## Today I feel:

## Write or draw anything about today

<table><tr><td>**Day**</td><td>**Date**</td></tr><tr><td>:</td><td>:</td></tr></table>

## I am thankful for:

1. _______________________________________________

2. _______________________________________________

3. _______________________________________________

**Who has made you happy today:**

## Today I feel:

## Write or draw anything about today

**Day**        **Date**

:            :

## I am thankful for:

⭐ **1** ______________________________________

⭐ **2** ______________________________________

⭐ **3** ______________________________________

**Who has made you happy today:**

## Today I feel:

## Write or draw anything about today

# Thank you.

We hope you enjoyed our journal.

As a small family company, your feedback is very important to us.

Please let us know how you like our journal at:

mollymcluke@gmail.com